INSPIRATIONAL
LIFE QUOTES
A Collection for your Daily Motivation

Alex Stephen

Author, Speaker, Transformation Coach

www.LifeTransformingTreasures.com

www.alexstephen.com

ISBN-10: 0991079728
ISBN-13: 978-0-9910797-2-8

www.alexstephen.com

3

ACKNOWLEDGEMENTS

Many thanks to the Divine Intelligence in the Universe that makes all things possible.

Thank you to the staff of Avocat Vedic Elementary School (Avocat/Fyzabad, Trinidad, West Indies). My journey started there under the guidance of my teachers and fearless leader, Principal Bickram Sawh, who always addressed me by my full name, Alexander Chandrabose Stephen.

Abundant blessings to every soul who helped me, with encouragement or deed, on this magnificent journey.

www.alexstephen.com

4

Declare this POWERFUL AFFIRMATION by filling in the blank:

I AM_____

YOU ARE the most powerful words, for what you put after them shapes your reality!

INTRODUCTION

My principal inspired my love for quotations. When I was a five-year-old boy, he planted the seeds of personal development in me. Beginning the morning assembly with quotes and stories, he empowered the students to excel in school and in life. Each classroom boasted motivational posters and banners and a famous quote, scripted with colorful chalk on a three-foot wide, one-foot high blackboard.

Principal Sawh's favorite quote, "Love Conquers All," was prominently displayed on the school's first floor. He often said that if we had health and wisdom, we could have anything we wanted in life. While in elementary school, I recorded quotations in a black notebook and read Dale Carnegie's personal development book, "How to Win Friends and Influence People."

www.alexstephen.com

Here is a joke my principal told frequently...

A fellow came back home to Trinidad, from studying in England. He hired a fisherman to take him out in the ocean for a ride. He asked the fisherman,

"Have you read Shakespeare?

When the fisherman replied, "No, I haven't," the fellow said, "Half of your life is gone."

"Have you read Chaucer?"

When the fisherman replied, "No, I haven't," the fellow repeated, "Half of your life is gone."

"Have you read the Vedas?"

Again, the fisherman replied, "No," and the fellow said, "Half of your life is gone."

And it went on and on.

www.alexstephen.com

7

Suddenly, there was a storm brewing. The fisherman turned a concerned gaze on his educated passenger and asked, "Can you swim?"

When the passenger replied, "No," the fisherman answered resolutely, "All of your life is gone!"

"Be Humble," Principal Bickram Sawh used to say. "Just be humble."

Mr. Sawh's stories and quotes have motivated me throughout my life. I yet maintain a notebook of great quotes, and now with the wide accessibility of the Internet, I share my favorite quotes with my large, Facebook following. Many of my social-media constituents have said the quotes I share have changed their lives exponentially.

I am honored to share this legacy of motivation with you. This book of my favorite quotes is dedicated to the following teachers who made a contribution and difference in my life:

www.alexstephen.com

8

Avocat Vedic Elementary School
(Avocat/Fyzabad, Trinidad, West Indies)

Mr. Bickram Sawh – Principal
Mr. B.C Rajkumar (Standard 4)
Mr. Sookdeo Manbodh (Standard 5)

Fyzabad Intermediate
(Anglican Secondary) (Fyzabad, Trinidad,
West Indies)

Mrs. Pearl Telemaque – Principal
Mr. Roland Ifill (Form Teacher 3rd–4th
and football)
Mr. Hubert Huggins (Form Teacher 5th
and cricket)

Iere High School
(Siparia, Trinidad, West Indies)

Reverend Cyril Beharry – Principal and
God Father
Mr. Patrick Jugmohansingh (Dean)
Mr. Ray Saney (Geography Form 6 and
Football–(Colleges Football League–1973
National Champions)

www.alexstephen.com

9

Mr. Deoraj Ramgoolam (Colleges Football League-1973 National Champions)

Howard University (Washington DC, USA)

Mr. Reginald Renwick (Recruiting)
Professor   Rackham   Goodlett (Mathematics)
Dr. Van Geeson (Accounting)

January 1ˢᵗ

"Unconditional love is powerful, and it is great to give and receive it."

~ Charisma Stephen

www.alexstephen.com

January 2nd

"When the student is ready, the teacher will appear."

~ Lao Tzu

January 3rd

"I expect to pass through the world but once. Any good therefore that I can do, or any kindness that I can show to my fellow creature, let me do it now. Let me not defer it or neglect it, for I shall not pass this way again."

~ William Penn

January 4*th*

"Don't let someone else's opinion of you become your reality."

~ Les Brown

January 5th

"When life knocks you down, try to land on your back. Because if you can look up, you can get up. Let your reason get you back up."

~ Les Brown

January 6th

"Carry out random acts of kindness with no expectation of reward, safe in the knowledge that one day someone might do the same for you."

~ Princess Diana

January 7th

"Progress is impossible without change, and those who cannot change their minds cannot change anything."

~ George Bernard Shaw

January 8th

"Life is too short…grudges
are a waste of perfect
happiness. Laugh when you
can, apologize when you
should and let go of what you
can't change."

~ Unknown

January 9th

"Without freedom from the past, there is no freedom at all."

~ J. Krishnamurti

January 10th

"How people treat you is their karma; how you react is yours."

~ Wayne W. Dyer

January 11th

"When you change the way you look at things, the things you look at change."

~ Wayne W. Dyer

January 12th

"I am realistic – I expect miracles."

~ Wayne W. Dyer

January 13th

"You'll see it when you believe it."

~ Wayne W. Dyer

January 14ᵗʰ

"Heaven is a state of mind,
not a location."

~ Wayne W. Dyer

January 15th

"It's never crowded along
the extra mile."

~ Wayne W. Dyer

January 16ᵗʰ

"You are living magnet.
What you attract into your
life is in harmony with
your dominant thought."

~ Brian Tracy

January 17ᵗʰ

"You don't pay the price of success. You pay the price of failure. You enjoy the benefits of success."

~ Zig Ziglar

www.alexstephen.com

January 18ᵗʰ

"Even if you are on the right track you will get run over if you just sit there."

~ Will Rogers

January 19ᵗʰ

"The defining factor for success is never resources; it's resourcefulness."

~ Tony Robbins

January 20th

"There is no "I" in team, but there is an "I" in win."

~ Michael Jordan

January 21st

"Tough times never last,
but tough people do."

~ Dr. Robert Schuller

January 22nd

"All achievements, all earned riches, have their beginning in an idea."

~ Napoleon Hill

January 23rd

"It is literally true that you can succeed best and quickest by helping others succeed."

~ Napoleon Hill

January 24^{*th*}

"Thoughts mixed with definiteness of purpose, persistence, and a burning desire are powerful things."

~ Napoleon Hill

January 25th

"Price is what you pay.
Value is what you get."

~ Warren Buffet

January 26th

"A dream is what you would like your life to become. A goal is what you are truly willing to do to achieve what you really want."

~ Denis Waitley

January 27ᵗʰ

"Let go of negative people
and positive ones will
appear."

~ Unknown

www.alexstephen.com

January 28th

"There is no passion to be
found in settling for a life
that is less than the one
you are capable of living."

~ Nelson Mandela

January 29th

"Forget past mistakes. Forget failures. Forget everything except what you're going to do now and do it."

~ William Durant

January 30ᵗʰ

"When your desires and belief are strong enough, you will appear to possess superhuman powers to achieve."

~ Napoleon Hill

January 31ˢᵗ

"Ask yourself – Where do I want to be one year from today? Personal growth is a choice."

~ Bob Proctor

February 1ˢᵗ

"Fire your boss by saying, "I've decided to go in another direction to live my dream, and not yours."

~ Les Brown

February 2nd

"Success is not the key to happiness. Happiness is the key to success. If you love what you are doing, you will be successful."

~ Herman Cain

February 3rd

"Success seems to be connected with action. Successful people keep moving. They make mistakes, but they don't quit."

~ Conrad Hilton

February 4ᵗʰ

"If you want to be happy,
set a goal that commands
your thoughts, liberates
your energy, and inspires
your hopes."

~ Andrew Carnegie

February 5th

"Many times we get so wrapped up in achieving our goals that we miss the opportunity to stop and be thankful for the things we have achieved."

~ T. D. Jakes

February 6ᵗʰ

"Change your thoughts and
you change your world."

~ Norman Vincent Peale

February 7th

"If you believe you can,
you probably can. If you
believe you won't, you
most assuredly won't.
Belief is the ignition switch
that gets you off the
launching pad."

~ Denis Waitley

February 8th

"It takes 20 years to build a reputation and five minutes to ruin it. If you think about that, you'll do things differently."

~ Warren Buffett

February 9th

"Your world is a living expression of how you are using and have used your mind."

~ Earl Nightingale

February 10th

"Stop acting as if life is a rehearsal. Live this day as if it were your last. The past is over and gone. The future is not guaranteed."

~ Wayne Dyer

February 11th

"Your future is created by what you do today, not tomorrow."

~ Robert Kiyosaki

February 12th

"Never reply when you are angry. Never make a promise when you are happy. Never make a decision when you are sad."

~ Anonymous

www.alexstephen.com

February 13th

"A teacher is never a giver of the truth; he is a guide, a pointer to the truth that each student must find for himself."

~ Bruce Lee

February 14th

"Those who dare to fail miserably can achieve greatly."

~ John F. Kennedy

February 15th

"If you don't like something, change it. If you can't change it, change your attitude."

~ Maya Angelou

February 16ᵗʰ

"A friend is someone who knows the song in your heart and can sing it back to you when you have forgotten the words."

~ Unknown

www.alexstephen.com

February 17th

"In the midst of movement and chaos, keep stillness inside of you."

~ Deepak Chopra

February 18th

"You cannot expect victory and plan for defeat."

~ Joel Osteen

February 19th

"It's easy to make a buck. It's a lot tougher to make a difference."

~ Tom Brokaw

February 20th

"No act of kindness, no matter how small, is ever wasted."

~ Aesop

February 21st

"Burn the bridge of Fear
and build your highway to
Success."

~ Raz Stephen

www.alexstephen.com

February 22nd

"Everyone may not be good, but there is always something good in everyone. Never judge anyone shortly because every saint has a past and every sinner has a future."

~ Oscar Wilde

February 23rd

"Through humor, you can soften some of the worst blows that life delivers."

~ Bill Cosby

February 24th

"It is one of the most beautiful compensations of this life that no man can sincerely try to help another without helping himself."

~ Ralph Waldo Emerson

February 25th

"No person was ever honored for what he received. Honor has been the reward for what he gave."

~ Calvin Coolidge

February 26th

"Believe, when you are most unhappy, that there is something for you to do in the world. So long as you can sweeten another's pain, life is not in vain."

~ Helen Keller

February 27ᵗʰ

"You will discover that you have two hands. One is for helping yourself and the other is for helping others."

~ Audrey Hepburn

February 28th

"As we express our gratitude, we must never forget that the highest appreciation is not to utter words, but to live by them."

~ John F. Kennedy

March 1ˢᵗ

"Gratitude opens the door to...the power, the wisdom, and the creativity of the universe. You open the door through gratitude."

~ Deepak Chopra

March 2nd

"The miracle of gratitude is that it shifts your perception to such an extent that it changes the world you see."

~ Dr. Robert Holden

March 3rd

"Let gratitude be the
pillow upon which you
kneel on to say your
nightly prayer."

~ Maya Angelou

March 4ᵗʰ

"If the only prayer you
said in your whole life was
"thank you" that will
suffice."

~ Miester Eckhart

March 5th

"When you practice gratefulness, there is a sense of respect toward others."

~ The Dali Lama

March 6th

"The best way to find you
is to lose yourself in the
service of others."

~ Gandhi

March 7ᵗʰ

"Nothing great was ever
achieved without
enthusiasm."

~ Emerson

March 8th

"The greatest good you can do for another is not just to share your riches, but to reveal to him his own."

~ Benjamin Disraeli

March 9th

"A friend is someone who knows all about you and still loves you."

~ Elbert Hubbard

March 10th

"Darkness cannot drive out darkness: only light can do that. Hate cannot drive out hate: only love can do that."

~ Martin Luther King Jr.

March 11th

"If you judge people, you have no time to love them."

~ Mother Teresa

March 12th

"Being deeply loved by someone gives you strength, while loving someone deeply gives you courage."

~ Lao Tzu

March 13th

"Not all of us can do great things. But we can do small things with great love."

~ Mother Teresa

March 14th

"One is loved because one is loved. No reason is needed for loving."

~ Paulo Coelho

March 15ᵗʰ

"Courage is grace under pressure."

~ Ernest Hemingway

March 16ᵗʰ

"Keep your fears to yourself, but share your courage with others."

~ Robert Louis Stevenson

March 17th

"We need a backbone, not a wishbone."

~ Joyce Meyer

March 18th

"Never interrupt someone
doing something you said
couldn't be done."

~ Amelia Earhart

March 19th

"A change is brought about because ordinary people do extraordinary things."

~ Barack Obama

March 20th

"If you don't like something, change it. If you can't change it, change your attitude."

~ Maya Angelou

March 21st

"What you seek is seeking
you."

~ Rumi

March 22ⁿᵈ

"A friend is someone who knows the song in your heart and can sing it back to you when you have forgotten the words."

~ Unknown

March 23rd

"Forgive others, not because they deserve forgiveness, but because you deserve peace."

~ Sufi Proverb

March 24ᵗʰ

"The only good is knowledge and the only evil is ignorance."

~ Socrates

March 25th

"If you are brave enough to say goodbye, life will reward you with a new hello."

~ Paulo Coelho

March 26th

"Gratitude is not only the greatest of virtues, but the parent of all others."

~ Marcus Cicero

March 27th

"Adversity causes some men to break and others to break records."

~ William Ward

March 28th

"You know how rich you are by counting the blessings in your life that money cannot buy."

~ Unknown

March 29th

"A great leader's courage to fulfill his vision comes from passion, not position."

~John Maxwell

March 30th

"To achieve happiness, we should make certain that we are never without an important goal."

~ Earl Nightingale

March 31st

"The quality of a person's life is in direct proportion to their commitment to excellence, regardless of their chosen field of endeavor."

~ Vince Lombardi

April 1st

"Humor is mankind's greatest blessing."

~ Mark Twain

April 2ⁿᵈ

"When you are living your passion, everything happens with ease, and the money follows you instead of you chasing the money."

~ Alex Stephen

April 3rd

"Your WHY drives you to greatness."

~ Raz Stephen

April 4th

"Persistence is the fuel that drives the engine of commitment."

~ Raz Stephen

April 5th

"One good thing about music, when it hits you, you feel no pain."

~ Bob Marley

April 6th

"In order to be successful you must rise before the sun."

~ James Stephen

April 7th

"Gratitude is the key that opens the door to your desires."

~Alex Stephen

April 8th

"We wish for you and your generations, a life of riches, peace, health and happiness."

~ Alex and Raz Stephen

April 9th

"The heart is happiest when it beats for others."

~ Unknown

April 10th

"Wear gratitude like a cloak and it will feed every corner of your life."

~ Rumi

April 11th

"Raise your words, not your voice. It is rain that grows flowers, not thunder."

~ Rumi

April 12th

"Lots of ways to reach
God, I chose love."

~ Rumi

April 13*th*

"The inspiration you seek
is already within you. Be
silent and listen."

~ Rumi

April 14ᵗʰ

"The man who asks a
question is a fool for a
minute; the man who does
not ask is a fool for life."

~ Confucius

\underline{www.alexstephen.com}

April 15ʰ

"Life is really simple, but
we insist on making it
complicated."

~ Confucius

April 16th

"Our greatest glory is not in ever falling, but in rising every time we fall."

~ Confucius

April 17th

"Choose a job you love, and you will never have to work a day in your life."

~ Confucius

April 18ᵗʰ

"Acknowledging the good that you already have in your life is the foundation for all abundance."

~ Eckhart Tolle

April 19th

"Worry pretends to be necessary, but serves no useful purpose."

~ Eckhart Tolle

April 20th

"Instead of asking 'What do I want from life?... a more powerful question is, 'What does life want from me?'"

~ Eckhart Tolle

April 21st

"Care about what other people think and you will always be their prisoner."

~ Lao Tzu

April 22nd

"New beginnings are often disguised as painful endings."

~ Lao Tzu

April 23rd

"He who controls others may be powerful, but he who has mastered himself is mightier still."

~ Lao Tzu

April 24ᵗʰ

"The journey of a
thousand miles begins with
a single step."

~ Lao Tzu

www.alexstephen.com

April 25ᵗʰ

"If you would take, you must first give; this is the beginning of intelligence."

~ Lao Tzu

April 26th

"Change your thoughts and
you change your world."

~ Norman Vincent Peale

April 27th

"Empty pockets never held anyone back. Only empty heads and empty hearts can do that."

~ Norman Vincent Peale

April 28ᵗʰ

"Live your life and forget
your age."

~ Norman Vincent Peale

April 29th

"Four things for success: work and pray, think and believe."

~ Norman Vincent Peale

April 30ᵗʰ

"Imagination is the true
magic carpet."

~ Norman Vincent Peale

May 1st

"If you cannot do great things, do small things in a great way."

~ Napoleon Hill

May 2nd

"Edison failed 10,000 times before he made the electric light. Do not be discouraged if you fail a few times."

~ Napoleon Hill

May 3rd

"Patience, persistence and perspiration make an unbeatable combination for success."

~ Napoleon Hill

May 4th

"The man who does more than he is paid for will soon be paid for more than he does."

~ Napoleon Hill

May 5ᵗʰ

"The ladder of success is never crowded at the top."

~ Napoleon Hill

May 6th

"The starting point of all achievement is desire."

~ Napoleon Hill

May 7th

"In the midst of movement
and chaos, keep stillness
inside of you."

~ Deepak Chopra

May 8th

"Be kind to yourself and others. Come from love every moment you can."

~ Deepak Chopra

May 9th

"I've learned that people will forget what you said, people will forget what you did, but people will never forget how you made them feel."

~ Maya Angelou

May 10th

"If you don't like something, change it. If you can't change it, change your attitude."

~ Maya Angelou

May 11ᵗʰ

"I've learned that making a 'living' is not the same thing as making a 'life.'"

~ Maya Angelou

May 12*th*

"Love recognizes no
barriers. It jumps hurdles,
leaps fences, penetrates
walls to arrive at its
destination full of hope."

~ Maya Angelou

May 13th

"Life is a gift, and I try to respond with grace and courtesy."

~ Maya Angelou

May 14th

"A bird doesn't sing because it has an answer, it sings because it has a song."

~ Maya Angelou

May 15th

"Success is to be measured not so much by the position that one has reached in life... as by the obstacles which he has overcome while trying to succeed."

~ Booker T. Washington

May 16th

"You can't hold a man down without staying down with him."

~ Booker T. Washington

May 17th

"I prayed for twenty years but received no answer until I prayed with my legs."

~ Frederick Douglass

May 18th

"You give but little when you give of your possessions. It is when you give of yourself that you truly give."

~ Kahlil Gibran

May 19th

"To be able to look back upon one's life in satisfaction is to live twice."

~ Kahlil Gibran

May 20ᵗʰ

"Yesterday is but today's memory; tomorrow is today's dream."

~ Kahlil Gibran

May 21ˢᵗ

"I prefer to be a dreamer among the humblest, with visions to be realized, than lord among those without dreams and desires."

~ Kahlil Gibran

May 22nd

"In the sweetness of friendship let there be laughter, and sharing of pleasures. For in the dew of little things the heart finds its morning and is refreshed."

~ Kahlil Gibran

May 23rd

"Love and doubt have never been on speaking terms."

~ Kahlil Gibran

May 24th

"Trust in dreams, for in them is hidden the gate to eternity."

~ Kahlil Gibran

May 25th

"Out of suffering have emerged the strongest souls; the most massive characters are seared with scars."

~ Kahlil Gibran

May 26th

"Be the change you want
to see in the world."

~ Gandhi

May 27th

"The best way to find yourself is to lose yourself in the service of others."

~ Gandhi

May 28th

"An ounce of practice is worth more than tons of preaching."

~ Gandhi

May 29th

"You may never know what results come of your action, but if you do nothing there will be no result."

~ Gandhi

May 30*th*

"Live as if you were to die tomorrow. Learn as if you were to live forever."

~ Gandhi

May 31ˢᵗ

"Happiness is when what you think, what you say, and what you do are in harmony."

~ Gandhi

June 1st

"You can't cross the sea merely by standing and staring at the water."

~ Rabindranath Tagore

June 2nd

"I slept and dreamt that life was joy. I awoke and saw that life was service. I acted and behold, service was joy."

~ Rabindranath Tagore

June 3rd

"Love is an endless mystery, for it has nothing else to explain it."

~ Rabindranath Tagore

June 4th

"Love does not claim possession, but gives freedom."

~ Rabindranath Tagore

June 5ᵗʰ

"Depth of friendship does not depend on length of acquaintance."

~ Rabindranath Tagore

June 6th

"Let me light my lamp," says the star. "And never debate if it will help to remove the darkness."

~ Rabindranath Tagore

June 7th

"He who is too busy doing good finds no time to be good."

~ Rabindranath Tagore

June 8th

"Everything comes to us that belongs to us if we create the capacity to receive it."

~ Rabindranath Tagore

June 9th

"Time is not measured by the passing of years but by what one does, what one feels, and what one achieves."

~ Jawaharlal Nehru

June 10th

"Life is like a game of cards. The hand you are dealt is determinism; the way you play it is free will."

~ Jawaharlal Nehru

June 11ᵗʰ

"Remember that failure is
an event, not a person."

~ Zig Ziglar

June 12th

"You will get all you want in life, if you help enough other people get what they want."

~ Zig Ziglar

June 13th

"People often say motivation doesn't last. Neither does bathing—that's why we recommend it daily."

~ Zig Ziglar

June 14th

"People don't buy for logical reasons. They buy for emotional reasons."

~ Zig Ziglar

June 15th

"Expect the best. Prepare for the worst. Capitalize on what comes."

~ Zig Ziglar

June 16th

"If you go looking for a friend, you're going to find they're scarce. If you go out to be a friend, you'll find them everywhere."

~ Zig Ziglar

June 17th

"A goal properly set is halfway reached."

~ Zig Ziglar

June 18th

"Your attitude, not your aptitude, will determine your altitude."

~ Zig Ziglar

June 19th

"If you can dream it, you can achieve it."

~ Zig Ziglar

June 20th

"You are the only person on earth who can use your ability."

~ Zig Ziglar

June 21st

"You were born to win, but to be a winner, you must plan to win, prepare to win, and expect to win."

~ Zig Ziglar

June 22ⁿᵈ

"You do not pay the price of success, you enjoy the price of success."

~ Zig Ziglar

June 23rd

"Some things you'll never know, and some things you will wish you never knew."

~ Dr. Eric E. Williams

June 24th

"If God had wanted us to live in a permissive society, He would have given us Ten Suggestions and not Ten Commandments."

~ Zig Ziglar

June 25th

"Failure is a detour, not a
dead-end street."

~ Zig Ziglar

June 26th

"Always bear in mind that your own resolution to succeed is more important than any one thing."

~ Abraham Lincoln

June 27th

"Better to remain silent
and be thought a fool than
to speak out and remove
all doubt."

~ Abraham Lincoln

June 28th

"I will prepare and someday my chance will come."

~ Abraham Lincoln

June 29th

"Nearly all men can stand adversity, but if you want to test a man's character, give him power."

~ Abraham Lincoln

June 30ᵗʰ

"You cannot escape the responsibility of tomorrow by evading it today."

~ Abraham Lincoln

July 1st

"I am easily satisfied with the very best."

~ Winston Churchill

July 2nd

"We are masters of the unsaid words, but slaves of those we let slip out."

~ Winston Churchill

July 3rd

"Courage is what it takes to stand up and speak; courage is also what it takes to sit down and listen."

~ Winston Churchill

July 4ᵗʰ

"Courage is going from failure to failure without losing enthusiasm."

~ Winston Churchill

July 5th

"Attitude is a little thing
that makes a big
difference."

~ Winston Churchill

July 6th

"We make a living by what
we get, we make a life by
what we give."

~ Sir Winston Churchill

July 7th

"There is no remedy for
love but to love more."

~ Henry David Thoreau

July 8th

"Do not lose hold of your dreams or aspirations. For if you do, you may still exist but you have ceased to live."

~ Henry David Thoreau

July 9ᵗʰ

"This world is but a canvas to our imaginations."

~ Henry David Thoreau

July 10th

"Wealth is the ability to fully experience life."

~ Henry David Thoreau

July 11ᵗʰ

"Live the life you've dreamed."

~ Henry David Thoreau

July 12th

"The smallest seed of faith is better than the largest fruit of happiness."

~ Henry David Thoreau

July 13th

"Live your beliefs and you
can turn the world
around."

~ Henry David Thoreau

July 14ᵗʰ

"Great minds discuss ideas; Average minds discuss events; Small minds discuss people."

~ Eleanor Roosevelt

July 15th

"No one can make you feel inferior without your consent."

~ Eleanor Roosevelt

July 16ᵗʰ

"Never allow a person to tell you no, who doesn't have the power to say yes."

~ Eleanor Roosevelt

July 17ᵗʰ

"It is better to light one small candle than to curse the darkness."

~ Eleanor Roosevelt

July 18ᵗʰ

"Women are like teabags. We don't know our true strength until we are in hot water!"

~ Eleanor Roosevelt

July 19th

"When you cease to make a contribution, you begin to die."

~ Eleanor Roosevelt

July 20th

"There are two ways to live: you can live as if nothing is a miracle; you can live as if everything is a miracle."

~ Albert Einstein

July 21ˢᵗ

"Logic will get you from A to B. Imagination will take you everywhere."

~ Albert Einstein

July 22nd

"Learn from yesterday, live for today, hope for tomorrow. The important thing is not to stop questioning."

~ Albert Einstein

July 23rd

"Insanity is doing the same thing over and over again and expecting different results."

~ Albert Einstein

July 24ᵗʰ

"It's not that I'm so smart, it's just that I stay with problems longer."

~ Albert Einstein

July 25ᵗʰ

"You have to learn the rules of the game. And then you have to play better than anyone else."

~ Albert Einstein

July 26ᵗʰ

"Imagination is everything.
It is the preview of life's
coming attractions."

~ Albert Einstein

July 27th

"The value of a man should be seen in what he gives and not in what he is able to receive."

~ Albert Einstein

July 28th

"Try not to become a man of success but rather to become a man of value."

~ Albert Einstein

www.alexstephen.com

July 29th

"If you can't feed a hundred people, then just feed one."

~ Mother Teresa

July 30ᵗʰ

"Courage is a love affair
with the unknown."

~ Osho

July 31ˢᵗ

"I never will understand all
the good that a simple
smile can accomplish."

~ Mother Teresa

August 1ˢᵗ

"A life not lived for others,
is not a life."

~ Mother Theresa

August 2nd

"I alone cannot change the world, but I can cast a stone across the waters to create many ripples."

~ Mother Theresa

August 3rd

"Within the child lies the fate of the future."

~ Maria Montessori

August 4th

"If you are humble nothing will touch you, neither praise nor disgrace, because you know what you are."

~ Mother Theresa

August 5th

"If you judge people, you have no time to love them."

~ Mother Theresa

August 6ᵗʰ

"I'm a little pencil in the hand of a writing God, who is sending a love letter to the world."

~ Mother Theresa

August 7th

"Kind words can be short and easy to speak, but their echoes are truly endless."

~ Mother Theresa

August 8th

"Live simply so others may simply live."

~ Mother Theresa

August 9th

"Peace begins with a smile."

~ Mother Theresa

August 10ᵗʰ

"Yesterday is gone.
Tomorrow has not yet
come. We have only today.
Let us begin."

~ Mother Theresa

August 11ᵗʰ

"Let no one ever come to you without leaving better and happier. Be the living expression of God's kindness: kindness in your face, kindness in your eyes, kindness in your smile."

~ Mother Theresa

August 12ᵗʰ

"The most important thing in communication is to hear what isn't being said."

~ Peter F. Drucker

August 13th

"The purpose of business is to create and keep a customer."

~ Peter F. Drucker

August 14th

"Follow effective action with quiet reflection. From the quiet reflection will come even more effective action."

~ Peter F. Drucker

August 15ᵗʰ

"Efficiency is doing things right; effectiveness is doing the right things."

~ Peter F. Drucker

August 16th

"Unless commitment is made, there are only promises and hopes; but no plans."

~ Peter F. Drucker

August 17ᵗʰ

"The only thing we know about the future is that it will be different."

~ Peter F. Drucker

August 18th

"Doing the right thing is more important than doing the thing right."

~ Peter F. Drucker

August 19ᵗʰ

"Be more concerned with your character than your reputation, because your character is what you really are, while your reputation is merely what others think you are."

~ John Wooden

August 20th

"Don't let what you cannot do interfere with what you can do."

~ John Wooden

August 21ˢᵗ

"Talent is God given. Be humble. Fame is man-given. Be grateful. Conceit is self-given. Be careful."

~ John Wooden

August 22nd

"If you don't have time to do it right, when will you have time to do it over?"

~ John Wooden

August 23ʳᵈ

"Ability may get you to the top, but it takes character to keep you there."

~ John Wooden

August 24ᵗʰ

"Never mistake activity for achievement."

~ John Wooden

August 25ᵗʰ

"Sports do not build character. They reveal it."

~ John Wooden

August 26th

"It's not so important who starts the game but who finishes it."

~ John Wooden

August 27ᵗʰ

"Young people need models,
not critics."

~ John Wooden

August 28th

"Be prepared and be honest."

~ John Wooden

August 29th

"I don't think you ever stop giving. I really don't. I think it's an on-going process. And it's not just about being able to write a check. It's being able to touch somebody's life."

~ Oprah Winfrey

August 30th

"Children are the world's most valuable resource and its best hope for the future."

~ John F. Kennedy

August 31ˢᵗ

"The more you praise and celebrate your life, the more there is in life to celebrate."

~ Oprah Winfrey

September 1st

"What God intended for
you goes far beyond
anything you can imagine."

~ Oprah Winfrey

September 2nd

"Where there is no struggle, there is no strength."

~ Oprah Winfrey

September 3rd

"The biggest adventure you can take is to live the life of your dreams."

~ Oprah Winfrey

September 4th

"Surround yourself with only people who are going to lift you higher."

~ Oprah Winfrey

September 5th

"You CAN have it all. You just can't have it all at once."

~ Oprah Winfrey

September 6ᵗʰ

"Be thankful for what you have; you'll end up having more. If you concentrate on what you don't have, you will never, ever have enough."

~ Oprah Winfrey

September 7th

"Passion is energy. Feel the power that comes from focusing on what excites you."

~ Oprah Winfrey

September 8th

"You know you are on the road to success if you would do your job, and not be paid for it."

~ Oprah Winfrey

September 9th

"The greatest discovery of all time is that a person can change his future by merely changing his attitude."

~ Oprah Winfrey

September 10th

"When I look into the future, it's so bright it burns my eyes."

~ Oprah Winfrey

September 11th

"It always seems impossible until it's done."

~ Nelson Mandela

September 12th

"The more positive you think, the more positive the outcome will probably be."

~ Nelson Mandela

September 13th

"Living isn't just about doing for yourself, but what you do for others as well."

~ Nelson Mandela

September 14ᵗʰ

"Life is a course with endless obstacles to hurdle."

~ Nelson Mandela

September 15ᵗʰ

"After climbing a great hill, one only finds that there are many more hills to climb."

~ Nelson Mandela

September 16th

"The greatest glory in living lies not in never falling, but in rising every time we fall."

~ Nelson Mandela

September 17th

"Keep your friends close
and your enemies closer."

~ Nelson Mandela

September 18th

"If you want to make
peace with your enemy,
you have to work with
your enemy. Then he
becomes your partner."

~ Nelson Mandela

September 19th

"Education is the most powerful weapon which you can use to change the world."

~ Nelson Mandela

September 20*th*

"There is no passion to be found playing small – in settling for a life that is less than the one you are capable of living."

~ Nelson Mandela

September 21st

"Money won't create success, the freedom to make it will."

~ Nelson Mandela

September 22nd

"Happiness belongs to the self-sufficient."

~ Aristotle

September 23rd

"Educating the mind without educating the heart is no education at all."

~ Aristotle

September 24th

"You never know how strong you are until being strong is your only choice."

~ Bob Marley

September 25th

"The greatness of a man is in his integrity and his ability to affect those around him positively."

~ Bob Marley

September 26th

"Even though we may be occupying one space, we are not able to communicate with each other."

~ Larry Stephen

www.alexstephen.com

September 27ᵗʰ

"Some people feel the rain.
Others just get wet."

~ Bob Marley

September 28th

"Free speech carries with it some freedom to listen."

~ Bob Marley

September 29th

"The difference between a successful person and others is not a lack of strength, not a lack of knowledge, but rather in a lack of will."

~ Vince Lombardi

September 30th

"Leaders aren't born, they are made. And they are made just like anything else, through hard work. And that's the price we'll have to pay to achieve that goal, or any goal."

~ Vince Lombardi

October 1st

"The measure of who we are is what we do with what we have."

~ Vince Lombardi

October 2nd

"Winning isn't everything, but the will to win is everything."

~ Vince Lombardi

October 3rd

"Life's battles don't always go to the stronger or faster man. But sooner or later the man who wins, is the man who thinks he can."

~ Vince Lombardi

October 4th

"Everything that irritates
us about others can lead
us to an understanding of
ourselves."

~ Carl Jung

October 5ᵗʰ

"Who looks outside,
dreams; who looks inside,
awakes."

~ Carl Jung

October 6th

"Move and the way will
open."

~ Zen Proverb

October 7th

"Those who know don't tell, and those who tell don't know."

~ Zen Proverb

October 8th

"Man can alter his life by altering his thinking."

~ William James

October 9th

"I don't sing because I'm happy; I'm happy because I sing."

~ William James

October 10th

"The sovereign cure for
worry is prayer."

~ William James

October 11ᵗʰ

"Action may not bring happiness but there is no happiness without action."

~ William James

October 12th

"I will love the light for it shows me the way, yet I will endure the darkness because it shows me the stars."

~ Og Mandino

October 13th

"Beginning today, treat everyone you meet as if they were going to be dead by midnight. Extend to them all the care, kindness, and understanding you can muster, and do it with no thought of any reward. Your life will never be the same again."

~ Og Mandino

October 14th

"Failure will never overtake me if my determination to succeed is strong enough."

~ Og Mandino

October 15th

"Work as though you would live forever, and live as though you would die today. Go another mile!"

~ Og Mandino

October 16th

"Ask not what your country can do for you; ask what you can do for your country."

~ John F. Kennedy

October 17ᵗʰ

"Let us never negotiate out of fear. But let us never fear to negotiate."

~ John F. Kennedy

October 18th

"Always seek out the seed of triumph in every adversity."

~ Og Mandino

October 19th

"Faith is taking the first step, even when you don't see the whole staircase."

~ Martin Luther King, Jr.

October 20th

"I submit to you that if a man hasn't discovered something he will die for, he isn't fit to live."

~ Martin Luther King, Jr.

October 21st

"I have learned it's always better to have a small percentage of a big success, than a hundred percent of nothing."

~ Art Linkletter

October 22nd

"Only in the darkness can
you see the stars."

~ Martin Luther King, Jr.

October 23rd

"Forgiveness is not an occasional act, it is a constant attitude."

~ Martin Luther King, Jr.

October 24th

"Coming together is a beginning. Keeping together is progress. Working together is success."

~ Henry Ford

October 25th

"Quality means doing it right when no one is looking."

~ Henry Ford

October 26th

"Whether you think that you can, or that you can't, you are usually right."

~ Henry Ford

October 27ᵗʰ

"Failure is simply the opportunity to begin again, this time more intelligently."

~ Henry Ford

October 28 th

"You can't build a
reputation on what you are
going to do."

~ Henry Ford

October 29th

"Don't find fault, find a remedy; anybody can complain."

~ Henry Ford

October 30th

"What lies behind you and
what lies in front of you,
pales in comparison to
what lies inside of you."

~ Ralph Waldo Emerson

October 31ˢᵗ

"Little minds have little worries; big minds have no time for worries."

~ Ralph Waldo Emerson

November 1st

"Be an opener of doors for such as come after thee."

~ Ralph Waldo Emerson

November 2nd

"Once you make a decision, the universe conspires to make it happen."

~ Ralph Waldo Emerson

November 3rd

"The only way to have a friend is to be one."

~ Ralph Waldo Emerson

November 4th

"Never lose an opportunity of seeing anything beautiful, for beauty is God's handwriting."

~ Ralph Waldo Emerson

November 5th

"Any person who
contributes to prosperity
must prosper in turn."

~ Earl Nightingale

November 6th

"You are, at this moment, standing right in the middle of your own acres of diamonds."

~ Earl Nightingale

November 7th

"All you have to do is know where you're going. The answers will come to you of their own accord."

~ Earl Nightingale

November 8th

"The key that unlocks energy is 'Desire.' It's also the key to a long and interesting life. If we expect to create any drive, any real force within ourselves, we have to get excited."

~ Earl Nightingale

November 9th

"We all walk in the dark and each of us must learn to turn on his or her own light."

~ Earl Nightingale

November 10ᵗʰ

"Excellence always sells."

~ Earl Nightingale

November 11th

"The big thing is that you know what you want."

~ Earl Nightingale

November 12th

"It isn't what you have, or who you are, or where you are, or what you are doing that makes you happy or unhappy. It is what you think about."

~ Dale Carnegie

November 13th

"Fear doesn't exist anywhere except in the mind."

~ Dale Carnegie

November 14*th*

"No man can become rich without himself enriching others."

~ Andrew Carnegie

November 15th

"There is little success where there is little laughter."

~ Andrew Carnegie

November 16th

"The first man gets the oyster, the second man gets the shell."

~ Andrew Carnegie

November 17ᵗʰ

"I would rather earn 1% off 100 people's efforts than 100% of my own efforts."

~ John D. Rockefeller

November 18th

"If you want to succeed you should strike out on new paths, rather than travel the worn paths of accepted success."

~ John D. Rockefeller

November 19ᵗʰ

"The most important thing for a young man is to establish credit – a reputation and character."

~ John D. Rockefeller

November 20*th*

"If you are aware that no one else can make you happy, and that happiness is the result of love coming out of you ...this is the Mastery of Love."

~ Don Miguel Ruiz

November 21st

"To one who has faith, no explanation is necessary. To one without faith, no explanation is possible."

~ St. Thomas Aquinas

November 22nd

"Faith is to believe what you do not see; the reward of this faith is to see what you believe."

~ Saint Augustine

November 23rd

"Patience is the companion
of wisdom."

~ Saint Augustine

November 24th

"When one door of happiness closes, another opens; but often we look so long at the closed door that we do not see the one which has been opened for us."

~ Helen Keller

November 25th

"The only thing worse than being blind is having sight but no vision."

~ Helen Keller

November 26th

"Keep your face to the
sunshine and you will
never see the shadow."

~ Helen Keller

November 27th

"The most beautiful things in the world cannot be seen or even touched; they must be felt with the heart."

~ Helen Keller

November 28th

"Compassion and tolerance
is not a sign of weakness,
but a sign of strength."

~ The Dalai Lama

November 29th

"Big things are expected
of us, and nothing big ever
came of being small."

~ Bill Clinton

November 30ᵗʰ

"You cannot change your destination overnight, but you can change your direction overnight."

~ Jim Rohn

December 1st

"You don't get paid for the hour. You get paid for the value you bring to the hour."

~ Jim Rohn

December 2nd

"Success is doing ordinary things extraordinarily well."

~ Jim Rohn

December 3rd

"Don't wish it were easier,
wish you were better."

~ Jim Rohn

December 4th

"Discipline is the bridge between goals and accomplishment."

~ Jim Rohn

December 5th

"The infinite intelligence in your subconscious can give you access to wonderful new kinds of knowledge."

~ Joseph Murphy

December 6th

"Make the most of every experience. Don't obsess over right and wrong decisions."

~ Deepak Chopra

December 7th

"Being ignorant is not so much a shame, as being unwilling to learn."

~ Benjamin Franklin

December 8th

"Courage is contagious. When a brave man takes a stand, the spines of others are often stiffened."

~ Billy Graham

December 9th

"The difference between extraordinary and ordinary is that little extra."

~ Jimmy Johnson

December 10th

"The end of your rope is the beginning of God's doorstep."

~ Unknown

December 11ᵗʰ

"Do what is right, not what
is easy."

~ John F. Kennedy

December 12th

"Evaluate the people in your life; then promote, demote or terminate, you are the CEO of your life."

~ Unknown

December 13ᵗʰ

"When your past calls do not answer, it has nothing new to say."

~ Unknown

December 14th

"I know God won't give me anything I can't handle. I just wish he didn't trust me so much."

~ Mother Theresa

December 15th

"Miracles start to happen
when you give as much
energy to your dreams as
you do to your fears."

~ Unknown

December 16ᵗʰ

"I am no longer accepting
the things I cannot change.
I am changing the things I
cannot accept."

~ Unknown

December 17th

"Go where you are celebrated – not tolerated. If they can't see the real value of you, it's time for a new start."

~ Unknown

December 18ᵗʰ

"You have never really lived until you do something for someone who can never repay you."

~ John Bunyan

December 19th

"Get on a Mission to live
your Passion!"

~ Alex Stephen

*December 20*th

"Kiss slowly, laugh insanely, love truly and forgive quickly."

~ Paulo Coelho

December 21ˢᵗ

"There is no pillow so soft
as a clear conscience."

~ French Proverb

December 22ⁿᵈ

"The happiness of your life depends on the quality of your thoughts."

~ Marcus Aurelius

December 23rd

"He is a wise man who does not grieve for the things which he has not, but rejoices for those which he has."

~ Epictetus

December 24th

"Expectation is the root of
all heartache."

~ William Shakespeare

December 25th

"Love all, trust a few, do wrong to none."

~ Shakespeare

December 26th

"The heart surrenders everything to the moment. The mind judges and holds back."

~ Ram Dass

December 27ᵗʰ

"One song can change a
moment, one idea can
change a world, one step
can start a journey but a
Prayer can change even
the impossible."

~ Unknown

December 28th

"The pessimist complains about the wind; the optimist expects change; the realist adjusts the sails."

~ William Ward

December 29ᵗʰ

"Leadership is based on inspiration, not domination; on cooperation, not intimidation."

~ William Ward

December 30ᵗʰ

"The point of power is always in the present moment."

~ Louise Hay

December 31ˢᵗ

"Life is not measured by the number of breaths we take but by the moments that take our breath away."

~ Unknown

CONCLUSION

"I hope you never lose your sense of
wonder,
You get your fill to eat but always keep
that hunger.
May you never take one single breath for
granted.
God forbid love ever leaves you empty
handed.
I hope you still feel small, when you stand
beside the ocean.
Whenever one door closes, I hope one
more opens.
Promise me that you'll give faith a fighting
chance,
And when you get the choice to sit it out
or dance,
I hope you dance. I hope you dance."

~ Lee Ann Womack~

www.alexstephen.com

STEPS TO IMPLEMENT

1. Gratitude

2. Journal

3. Charity

4. Meditation

5. Exercise

6. Diet

7. Spirituality

8. Discipline

9. Integrity

10. Character

www.alexstephen.com

"Good luck, my friends. I hope these

quotes lift you and prove

transformative on your journey!

~Alex Stephen~

President and CEO

Life Transforming Treasures Corp

www.alexstephen.com

WHAT OTHERS ARE SAYING

"I love your generosity of spirit & wisdom. It is really your quotes. They start the ball rolling. I enjoy them immensely."

"Alex, you are the CIO, Chief Inspiration Officer. You got me through a lot of difficult times."

"You are a true sage & a godly man sent to enrich & guide my life! Your quotes have taught me to appreciate all things in my life, and now I am living a life of Gratitude."

"Thank you, Alex, for unknowingly motivating me. Thanks for your generosity."

"I have been fascinated and enthralled by the positive quotes you share. Sir, please keep doing the same. Good luck to you. Keep motivating the world. It's required!"

www.alexstephen.com

"Every time I read your quotes and see the pictures, it takes me to a place I'd love to be."

"Happiness is contagious, and you make very, very happy. Keep it up. You are awe inspiring!"

"It's nice to see someone keeping it 100% positive all of the time. Continue giving daily inspiration the way God leads you. It's helping someone somewhere. I promise you. I love your posts; they inspire me!"

"You uplift us with your positive quotes & insights! Quite inspiring. Continue your great works full of light!"

"I always found your quotes to be Inspiring, Encouraging and Excellent Reminders of life. There were times when I could not wait to read your posts, especially when I felt the "world coming down" on me, and, at those times, I always depended on your "pick me up" posts. They encouraged me and made me

www.alexstephen.com

381

a stronger, more open-minded person. Thank you. God Bless!"

"I find inspiration and strength in many of your quotes. This is a service for humanity. So, my friend, live it, speak it, feel it, think it, share it & be it, just as you imagine your heart's desire from the Highest."

"This is your Gift! Your post & position reflect your bright, sunny WORLD & for me this is Great! THANKS FOR YOUR LIGHT & CONTINUE TO RISE!"

"Your quotes on FB are very helpful. There are times when I don't feel myself, for whatever reason, and I just happen to see something you posted. It suits exactly my situation at the time. You are a great inspiration, and I love your posts."

"I love your quotes. They lift me and remind me that thinking positive during my day can change my attitude and the attitude of others. We need more love and positivism in the world today."

www.alexstephen.com

"You're doing a great job; touching people's lives is a real blessing. You have a healing touch!"

THE POWER OF THE SPOKEN WORD

"Avoid foul-mouthed people. If you're one of them, commit to lose this part of yourself. Don't allow yourself to be a vessel or a sponge for filthy, disrespectful language or a garbage disposal for violent words, especially toward people whom you are supposed to love.

Some people enjoy using profanity, even when talking to or in the presence of children. Many people pay to listen to foul-mouthed rappers, comedians and various entertainers. However, to accept this as normal only speaks to our loss of spirituality and self-respect. It highlights the tragic lowering of our standards for language which has negatively impacted our children.

Cursing is the strongest expression of a weak mind. Don't fool yourself! Life and death are in the tongue. Your words

www.alexstephen.com

create your world, and your world reflects your reality. You always have a choice. Use words that represent the highest and best expression of yourself and of what you see for your future and your life. You deserve it!"

~Les Brown~

NOTES:

NOTES:

LINKS AND CONTACTS

The Stephen Family can be reached at the following links and contacts:

http://www.LifeTransformingTreasures.com

www.LifeTransformingTreasures.com

Free Personal Developmental Products

www.personaldevelopmentpowerpack.com

www.NextLevelRiches.com ~ A home-study

training system with video, audio,

PDF and worksheets

Free Strategy Session www.meetwithalex.com

http://www.LTT7.com/guide

www.LTT7.com/guide ~ Transformation Coaching

on a one-on-one basis

info@alexstephen.com

www.alexstephen.com

Mail To:
Life Transforming Treasures Corporation
P.O. Box 157
Marlboro, MA 01752
USA

www.alexstephen.com

389

RAZ AND ALEX STEPHEN

www.alexstephen.com

www.alexstephen.com

391

ABOUT THE AUTHOR

Alex Stephen has faced and overcome many challenges in his life, and because he has turned his tragedies into triumphs, he now draws on his lessons and experiences to help others.

Alex graduated from Howard University with a Bachelor in Business Administration (BBA) Magna Cum Laude. A Certified Public Accountant (CPA), he built a 20-year career in business finance where he held titles such as Corporate Loan Officer and Vice President/Director. He has worked in public and private companies.

As a young man, Alex had the opportunity to work in his grandfather's businesses. As a result, he learned to work with a wide variety of people with different personalities and values and from different backgrounds. This experience, coupled with his spiritual upbringing, enabled him to develop a strong intuition

www.alexstephen.com

in evaluating life situations. Long before Alex became a transformation coach, his friends, fellow students, and co-workers sought his advice. He believes this has been his experience, in part, because he helps people get results quickly.

Today, Alex lives his passion by helping people transform their lives. Guiding and empowering them to reach their goals and fulfill their life's purpose, he helps his clients to identify their pain, accept where they are, and create plans to get to their desired destination. In addition, he contributes much of his success to the following eclectic teaching strategies: transformation coaching, motivational speaking, and authoring of multi-media materials such as books, CD's, workbooks, podcasts, social media and videos.

Alex, his wife Raz, and their children, Larry and Charisma, wrote their first book: *"Courage in our Hearts ™...A Family's Love Story."*

www.alexstephen.com

Alex is an author, speaker and transformation coach, who strives to elevate everyone he meets. His life is an example of how to live your purpose and create a legacy for your loved ones.

www.alexstephen.com

Greetings, Reader,

If you enjoyed reading this book, please write a review on Amazon.

Thank you,

Alex

www.alexstephen.com

11697159R00223

Made in the USA
San Bernardino, CA
26 May 2014